G000126246

TED LEECH

summersdale

REALLY GROSS FACTS

Summersdale Publishers Ltd
46 West Street
Chichester
West Sussex
PO19 1RP
UK

www.summersdale.com

Printed and bound in Great Britain

ISBN 1 84024 474 7

REALLY GROSS FACTS

Contents

Introduction

We've gathered the foulest, grossest, most revolting facts to disgust and delight you. Read on to discover what farts are made of, what fast food employees *really* get up to and what's more horrible than choking on your own vomit...

Caution: Do not read at meal times.

REALLY GROSS BODY FACTS

Vomit is an interesting
cocktail of partially
digested food,
mucus, saliva, acids
and chemicals.

If you share food such as chips or sweets with anyone you have a 1% chance of eating some of their faeces.

REALLY
GROSS
FACTS

Sleeping on your
right side makes
you burp and snore
at the same time,
because it is easier
for gas to escape
from your stomach.

When you inhale, the air enters your nose at 4 mph, although it rushes in at 20 mph when you take a good sniff. When you sneeze, the air speeds out of your nose at 100 mph.

You don't sweat evenly
under each arm;
right-handed people
sweat more under
their left arm, and
it's the right armpit
that gets sweatier for
left-handed people.

Frequent users of heroin find that, after a while, their veins become too hard and they have to find new places to inject their happy drug. They inject into less-obvious veins such as those in their groin, feet, neck or under their tongues.

If one person farted
continually for 81
months, they would
produce the same
amount of energy
as a nuclear bomb.

If you were stabbed, your blood would squirt out of your body to land up to 9 metres away due to the pressure created by your heart as it beats.

Every year you will
shake hands with
11 women who have
recently masturbated
and failed to wash
their hands…

… but with only 6 men over the same period.

REALLY
GROSS
FACTS

In doing ordinary
things like using a
shared computer,
pulling out a chair
to sit on or holding
onto the handrail on
the bus, your hands
will come into indirect
contact with 15
penises in one day.

During your life, 22 painters, plumbers and electricians will take a look in your dirty washing bin.

Every time you go to
a wedding reception,
you have a 1% chance
of getting a cold sore
from another guest.

You inhale 1 litre of other people's fart gases every day.

Women fart 3 times
more during the
day than men do.

You have 250,000 pores on your feet, and they produce a quarter of a cup of sweat every single day.

Your mouth has a population of over one million microscopic creatures.

Dust is made up of the ten billion tiny scales of dead skin that you shed every day. That's equivalent to 18 bags of flour over your whole life.

Your skin and your spit contain more bacteria than your urine.

50% of women and more than 90% of men do not wash their hands after they have been to the toilet unless someone else is watching them.

The germs in your faeces are surprisingly resilient; they can eat their way through a stack of ten sheets of paper.

GROSS
FACTS

The record holder for
projectile vomiting
managed to disgorge
the contents of his
stomach to a distance
of 8 metres.

Over 1 ton of pubic
hair is extracted
from water treatment
plants every month.

The microscopic parasites that live on your body make up 0.01% of your weight.

The biggest tapeworm
ever found inside
the human body was
33 metres long.

Farts are caused by three major factors; chemical reactions, gas from our blood that escapes into our intestines and air that we swallow. People that eat a lot of foods such as meat, cauliflower and eggs are likely to have the smelliest farts because these foods are full of the stinky gas sulphur.

REALLY
GROSS
FACTS

There is a 50% chance
that your washing
machine contains
traces of faeces.

Earwax, or cerumen, comes in many interesting varieties; not only can you find different colours, including yellow, brown and grey, but also different textures. Some people have moist, sticky wax inside their ears, while others produce wax of a much drier consistency.

Over your lifetime, you will produce enough spit to fill a swimming pool.

Morticians have to do a special type of massage on the stomachs of dead bodies in order to release any gas that may be trapped in the abdomen.

Human faeces contain germs and bacteria as well as over 100 types of virus.

Belly button fluff is made from clothing fibres that stick to the sweat that your body produces, and stay tucked inside your belly button even after the sweat has dried.

There are lots of tiny bacteria that enjoy feasting on the sweat that your feet produce, and it's their excrement as well as the dead bacteria that produces the gunk between your toes and makes your feet pong.

Albert Einstein may have left
this earth, but his brain is
still here. Parts of it were
stolen after he died and, over
the years, fragments have
been sold to Einstein fans all
over the world. His eyeballs
were pickled, placed in a
display jar and auctioned off
to the highest bidder, while
it is rumoured that some
of his internal organs were
also taken and may be in the
hands of private collectors.

If you put a stainless-steel spoon in a pot of the hydrochloric acid that's in your stomach, it would dissolve before your very eyes.

If it wants to come out, it will; you can't prevent yourself from vomiting by keeping your mouth shut — it will come out of your nose instead.

Your underwear can be contaminated with up to 10 grams of poo-related material.

Your stomach needs to produce a lining of mucus every 2 weeks to stop it digesting itself.

The longest recorded
fart lasted 2 minutes
and 42 seconds.

Your loofah contains more bacteria than your toilet, and your kitchen is home to more germs than your bathroom.

REALLY
GROSS
FACTS

When Eskimo
babies have colds,
their mothers
suck the snot out
of their noses

There's a scientific term for nose picking — rhinotillexomania.

There have been many recorded incidents of people being suffocated at theme parks when they puke on a roller-coaster that is going so fast that the vomit is plastered to their faces and they can't breathe. It's a gross way to die, but it's even grosser when the vomit isn't yours…

REALLY

GROSS

INSECT AND

ANIMAL

FACTS

When a skipper caterpillar spots the arrival of a predator, such a wasp, it shoots pellets of poo out of its rear end at almost two metres a second! This is because wasps love the smell of these bum bullets so much that they'll fly after them, leaving the caterpillar in peace.

Every year 14 bugs find their way into your mouth while you sleep, and yes, you do swallow most of them.

REALLY
GROSS
FACTS

Female racehorses
have their labia sewn
shut at the beginning
of their careers to
'streamline' their
bodies in an attempt
to make them run as
fast as possible.

Park lawns in London are watered by over 1 million gallons of dog urine every single year.

Cockroaches release methane when they are alive, but also for up to 18 hours after they die.

Flies are sick every time they land — sometimes they eat the vomit but mostly they just leave it. And they're not fussy about the location for ejecting the contents of their stomachs, they will do it on food, skin, knives, forks…

Ever wondered about the
life cycle of worms? It goes
something like this: the
eggs are laid in warm, moist
conditions such as soil or
a bowl of cat food. The cat
eats the eggs, and when the
worms hatch, they travel
through the cat's body by
way of the intestine, blood
stream, liver and windpipe.
Once inside the throat of the

cat, they are swallowed and move into the intestine again where they grow into adults and lay their own eggs. The white stuff that you find around cats' bottoms is the end of the worm containing the eggs. When the white tail of the worm bursts, the eggs are released, ready to begin the cycle all over again.

Cockroaches lurk in bathrooms and kitchens because they're attracted to moisture. However, there is one type of cockroach that looks elsewhere to find the moist conditions that it so enjoys – people's faces. They are attracted to eyes

as these are the source of
all sorts of minerals — they
nibble on the eyelashes as
well as drinking the salty
water from the tear ducts.
Others prefer to head
to the nose to find tasty
snacks up the nostrils.

How do you kill a cockroach? By chopping off its head. After 9 days it will finally die... of starvation.

Plant-eating animals such as rabbits eat their own faeces because they can't fully digest the plants the first time.

Dogs eat cat faeces
because it is high
in protein.

Pinworms are a type of parasite that hatch inside your body. They lay their eggs on your anus making it itch. If you scratch the itch and then put your fingers in your mouth, the eggs can be transferred into your body where they live happily ever after.

Cockroaches fart
every 15 minutes.

Female cochineal
beetles are ground
to produce a dye
that is used in some
juices, sweets and
beauty products.

Every cockroach
carries the bacteria for
40 different diseases,
including the plague
and hepatitis.

The Romans used
crushed mouse brains
as toothpaste.

REALLY
GROSS
FACTS

In the Middle Ages, women smeared cat faeces on their faces to get rid of unwanted hair.

REALLY GROSS TORTURE FACTS

When it comes to torture, the Chinese have always been extremely imaginative. They punished monks who broke their vows by burning holes through their necks and pulling a metal chain through the hole. After that, they

forced the unfortunate monk
to walk through the streets
with his new piercing trailing
behind him. If he lifted up
the chain to gain even the
briefest moment of rest from
the agony, they whipped him.

In France they used animals to inflict torture on people. They covered a victim's feet in salt and then brought in goats to lick them clean. This was because a goat's tongue is extremely rough so eventually the skin of the unfortunate person's feet was rubbed off. The salt was reapplied on a regular basis.

If your head is chopped off, your brain will keep functioning for around 15 seconds after your head and body have parted company.

During the French Revolution
after an aristocrat was
beheaded, their flesh was
used to bind books, even
though the flesh rotted quite
quickly and artists gathered
the blood from around
the guillotine to use as a
paint substitute in creating
their masterpieces. Some

museums in France display these gory paintings today. This fleshy fad extended to the nineteenth century when Charles Dickens had a bookmark made from the skin of William Burke, a mass murderer who was executed in 1829.

Henry II died after his lover got mad and pushed a burning poker up his anus.

Henry VIII's favourite form of punishment for poisoners was boiling them alive. The first victim of this steamy execution was a chef who had added a diarrhoea-inducing herb to one of his dishes. Two diners died and Henry VIII ordered the chef to be boiled in his own pot.

Mary Queen of Scot's beheading did not quite go to plan: the first swing of the executioner's axe only cut the side of her neck slightly. The second didn't manage to completely sever the neck from the body so the executioner had to complete the job with a saw. When he picked up the head to display it to the audience, he inadvertently grabbed the wig she'd been wearing and dropped the head making it bounce across the floor.

After tying him to a tree, shooting him with arrows and then cutting him open to remove his lungs, the Vikings finished off their grisly murder of King Edmund of England by chopping off his head.

Another King Edmund
met a nasty end
in 1016, when an
assassin with a dagger
hid in the hole that
served as the toilet.
You can guess where
the dagger went…

The English used a torture instrument called the barnacles. It was a stick with a little noose on one end into which the victim's upper lip was placed. They tightened the noose around the lip and twisted the stick to contort the lip in all sorts of unnatural ways.

REALLY GROSS STORIES

After being shot in the head with a nail gun, a young man from Texas went to the hospital complaining of a bad headache. When doctors examined the X-ray, they found that an eight-centimetre nail was lodged in his brain and had gone in with such force that even

the head of the nail was
inside his skull. Amazingly,
after doctors performed
an eight-hour operation to
remove the nail, he survived.
The only after-effects of
the accident were that he
had trouble remembering
things and he no longer
liked American Football.

In Australia a milk farmer was busy going about her job when her hair got caught in a machine in the milking shed, taking one of her ears, and her face, with it. Medics unhooked her face from the machine and rushed her to hospital where she underwent a 25-hour operation, involving several surgeons and 30 pints of blood. She survived and, apart from a few scars, looked pretty much as she had done before.

An office worker in America died after biting off the dry skin on his foot and choking on it.

When a lorry containing pig intestines and other pig parts overturned on a busy Yorkshire motorway on its way to a local factory, the local fire brigade was called out to clean up the mess. A pump was used to clean up the chunkier bits but the unfortunate firemen had to shovel and sweep the rest of the mess into rubbish bags.

93

When rescue workers got
to the scene of a steam
train crash, they found
that the engineer, who
had been driving the train,
had been thrown clear of
the wreckage. It wasn't
the impact or the fall that
had killed him, but the

steam from the boiler.
The crash had caused the
highly pressurised boiler
to explode, releasing all
the steam and scalding
the engineer to death. The
force of the steam actually
removed all of the hair on
his head and upper body.

A Russian woman fell
in a sinkhole (a pool of
boiling mud and water
that forms under roads
and buildings) whilst
shopping in her village
and, despite attempts
by passers-by to pull
her out, she was boiled
to death in the mud.

While celebrating his wedding night to drunken excess, Attlia the Hun passed out, got a nosebleed, and choked to death on the blood.

REALLY
GROSS
FACTS

There are many reported cases of people's intestines being sucked out of their bodies by the power of the flush on aeroplane toilets. But did you know that the intake holes in swimming pools are just as dangerous? Some pools have only one hole for water to be pumped out for recirculation and these holes have extremely strong suction and can pull your intestines out of your body. One woman survived such an encounter even though she lost almost 6 feet of these vital organs.

REALLY
GROSS
FACTS

An extremely overweight woman was taken to hospital complaining of stomach pains. The cause of these pains was initially diagnosed as an abscess, but further investigation showed that the abscess was actually caused by her remote control, which had gotten lost between her mounds of flesh after she sat on it.

Despite numerous consultations, doctors failed to diagnosis a bowel obstruction in a young boy. When the eleven year old finally passed away after his agonising illness, he weighed just 45 pounds. The post mortem revealed that 22 pounds of that was faecal matter that had been building up inside his bowels.

A woman who had slimmed down from 20 stone to just 10 after a stomach stapling operation was really pleased with her new body. However, she was a bit concerned about a hard lump extending from her belly button. The doctor removed and examined the lump, and found that it was made of compressed belly button fluff that she hadn't noticed before when her stomach was so fat.

Two weeks after returning
from a visit to Peru, a
man went to his doctor
complaining of extreme pain
in his right ear, as well as
constant queasiness and
strange noises that seemed
to be coming from inside
his head. Surgery revealed

that a spider, which must have crawled into his ear during his trip, had eaten through his eardrum, causing the pain, and was making itself at home within his head, causing the noises. Surgeons also found some spider eggs…

REALLY

GROSS

FooD AND
DRINK

FACTS

If you go to China,
be careful what you
order in restaurants
— rats are a very
popular dish and can
be found on many
menus in a variety of
serving suggestions:

Deep-fried rat is
a speciality.

They add chunks of
roasted rat to soup.

Boiled rat accompanied
by slices of snake is
highly recommended.

A double delight is 2 rats, individually wrapped in banana leaves and steamed.

Exploring the great outdoors
can be an adventure. But
beware: water hemlock
may look like a carrot or
a parsnip but it causes
incredibly painful stomach
cramps followed by
convulsions that gradually
get worse until you're
seizing uncontrollably.
Then you'll start to vomit
incessantly although you
may be lucky enough to just

heave between convulsions.
Next you'll go blind and
begin to froth at the mouth.
Meanwhile, the convulsions
will continue and will
eventually get so strong that
your back could break, after
which you'll probably lose
consciousness. The green
stomach bile will continue
to froth from your mouth
even after you're dead.

The next time you're munching into your favourite fast food burger, remember that some people have had extra gross additions to their meals: whole chicken heads, rat body parts, live insects and even maggots have been reported by unlucky customers.

If you consume takeaways on a regular basis, you will swallow about 12 pubic hairs every year.

Fast-food restaurant employees have admitted to spraying oven cleaner onto burgers, and taking food into the toilets to add their own flavouring.

You swallow half a litre of urine during a 60-minute swim.

450 grams of peanut butter can contain up to 150 insect body parts and 5 rat hairs.

Instead of popcorn, cinemas in Columbia offer their customers a snack of deep-fried ant bodies.

Think about this next time someone offers to make you a cup of tea: E.coli has been found on 10% of mugs.

Renowned for its aphrodisiac properties, Khoona is reserved by Afghani tribesmen for their wedding nights. This special drink is freshly-extracted (and warm) bull semen.

Canned drinks contain
2 tablespoons of
your saliva.

The Tudors believed that drinking a pint of ale containing 9 head lice would cure liver problems. They also thought that applying squashed beetles to the head would promote hair growth and that swallowing butter-coated baby frogs would help asthma sufferers.

The Roman Emperor
Claudius had huge feasts
with so much food that
people couldn't continue
eating until they had
thrown up. They made
their slaves tickle their
throats to force them to
empty their stomachs,
freeing them up for
the next course.

Also Available

BORED
Stupid!

Brainless things to do when you're bored

A. FIDGET

BORED STUPID

A. FIDGET

£2.99

Paperback

Sand a mushroom... Ring McDonald's and complain about the food... Write a book about a previous life... Polish the ceiling... Plait your dog's hair... Wash a tree.

Bored to tears? On the bus, in a lecture, at home or at work, let's face it: life can be mind-numbingly boring sometimes.

Brighten up your drab and wholly pointless life with these brainless and completely daft things to do.

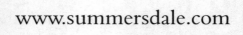

www.summersdale.com